the ones who keep quiet

the ones who keep quiet
DAVID HOWARD

'Are you listening to the ones who keep quiet?'
– Joseph Joubert (1791)

OTAGO

Published by Otago University Press
Level 1, 398 Cumberland Street
Dunedin, New Zealand
university.press@otago.ac.nz
www.otago.ac.nz/press

First published 2017
Copyright © David Howard

The moral rights of the author have been asserted.
ISBN 978-0-947522-44-5

Editor: Emma Neale
Design/layout: Fiona Moffat

Cover image: Stephen Ellis, *The Anchor Drags* (2014). Ballpoint pen and correction fluid on
paper, 1120 x 1560mm. Collection of the James Wallace Arts Trust, Auckland. Stephen Ellis is
represented by Sanderson Contemporary.

Author photo: Dean Nixon

Printed in New Zealand by Printlink, Wellington.

CONTENTS

Acknowledgements

Some of these poems first appeared in: *Contrappasso*, *Cordite*, *JAAM*, the *Journal of Stevenson Studies*, *Landfall*, *Otago Daily Times*, *The Speak House* (Lyttelton: Cold Hub Press, 2014), *Takahē*, *Truck*, and *you're so pretty when you're unfaithful to me* (Auckland: Holloway Press, 2012). I am grateful to Roger Hickin and Peter Simpson for their faith in my work.

A trip to Vienna to research Andreas Reischek was shaped by the kindness of Esther Dischereit, Gudrun Kollegger and the Winter family: Jacqueline, Leo, Maia and Martin. A related trip to Britain was supported by Renate Hayes and Fabian Williges, Douglas Pike, and Daniel and Georgie Meadows.

This collection was drafted over several residencies:
The Robert Burns Fellowship (2013) at the University of Otago; I tip my hat to the Department of English & Linguistics.
The Otago Wallace Residency (2014) at the Pah Homestead, sponsored by Sir James Wallace and the University of Otago.
A UNESCO City of Literature Residency in Prague (2016), which was enriched by Katerina Bajo, Marta Jirácková, Liz Knowles, Radka Navarová, Tomas Mika, David Vaughan and the Municipal Library of Prague.
The Ursula Bethell Fellowship 2016 at the University of Canterbury; I thank Julia and Vic Allen, Pieta Gray and Nicholas Wright for their camaraderie.

The Ghost of James Williamson 1814–2014

'What forsworn ghost of the family is now played at through this
approximating violence?'

– Matthew Wood: F4: *In the Interval*

1   Before 22 March 1888

You never know. To come up
  an anchor must go down down down
      where light is forbidden
      and the largest things are hidden
  with the smallest. If sailors drown
their teeth fill a cup

made of coral. They're empty
  like fishing nets twisted again
      and again. We all sink
      into our element yet think
  nothing of it – that's the *Amen*
a drowned man must be.

But I did not drown. And out
  beyond the horizon a child
      stares at, I am walking
      starboard with the master, talking
  through coordinates, reconciled
beyond any doubt

we are off course, despite cross
  after cross on a foreign chart
      justifying the ways
      of men to men. The longest days
  the shortest nights, I'm one more part
of God's cosmic loss.

There's no place like homelessness
    because it gets under the skin.
        But inarticulate
        things – they shift with every minute,
    it takes words to plumb what's within
then fix it. I guess

I was lost for years and years.
    The parts of speech make an anchor
        hanging off each person.
        And the parts of an anchor, crown
    flukes palms shank ring and stock, they're for
holding what appears

to move perpetually.
    We need to *speak* to feel alive
        in silence. The chief mate
        from Sydney, I've shifted as freight
    shifts in the hold. I will arrive
a changed man, clearly

one condemned to eternal
    return. I gaze over the bow,
        bobbing in the cosmos.
        On a four o'clock watch the loss
    of perspective gets to you: how
the ship is in thrall

to foam that's boiling over
    the bulwarks, its jib-boom dipping
        under a hopeless gale;
        two lower topsails, reefed foresail
    taking the strain, you are slipping
into the lower

realm, cast out of your body.
    Come heavy weather every man's
        flung from a bunk, swearing
        by his god, with the waves bearing
    down down down on those best laid plans,
sky swallowed by sea.

Stunned underneath the Gothic
    arch of a monstrous swell, I reach
        towards an afterthought –
        the *unreal* becomes our last port
    of call. The only way to teach
others is to stick

to our core business, living
    well, until the loudest breaker
        takes every breath away
        and there is neither night nor day;
    to quickly dismiss our Maker –
there's no forgiving

death when our ship rounds Cape Brett
    to the Bay of Islands' new world.
        If some of us must grope
        through the dark, out of heart and hope,
    now each leaf is a flag unfurled
so we won't forget

the Old Country's bloody laws.
    Our fall *into* Paradise shows
        God is an ironist
        who gives the knife another twist –
    pointed refusal to disclose
proof He's the First Cause,

here. At Kororareka
    I gave up the sea that gave up
        so many nameless men,
          selling rum to tattoos again
    when barques put in. Jack Tars would cup
their hands and pucker

blistered lips for service: 'Half-
    starved, grass-fed nag that you are, trot
        over here with a drop!'
          After a year I shut up shop
    and bought a quarter-acre lot
in Auckland. My rough

plan? To speculate in land
    and become Machiavelli's
        Antipodean prince,
          cultivating more than silence.
    My father ran two companies
in Belfast, I'm damned

by his words: 'Beat that, young man.'
    I tried for his success with sails
        but lost faith when the waves
          shrugged their shoulders. No one behaves
    well if their family curtails
choices. While you scan

the horizon, taste vomit
    thinking of what reputation
        you have left, how it fits
          inside a kit bag. The earth splits
    in two, as if the Creation
failed, a long comet

lost in space. I'll navigate
    mortgages the way a pilot
        plays sandbars at low tide,
        knowing where and when you can ride
    a current. I'll float in private
on currency's late

surge but publicly deny
    my ambition. I'll *serve* Auckland
        on the arm of my wife
        Julia, her eyes hold my life
    to come, they are diamonds and
blue … 'James, wave goodbye!'

I heard my late father yell
    after midnight. And morning brought
        the footfall of bailiffs,
        their faces set like bull mastiffs
    ready to attack. I was caught
by the ankle, fell

arse over kite. Once Auckland
    Agricultural Company
        collapsed – a circus tent
        floated on hot air – government
    of all my faculties left me.
Pah was built on sand

 as proof the earth inherits
    meek and strong alike. Puriri,
        southern magnolia,
        London plane, Hill's grevillia,
    Chilean wine palm, hackberry –
they shadow us, bits

of the Paradise that was
　　lost before I cut my eye teeth
　　　　upon weevils. 'Goodbye!'
　　　　　echoes my old man and the sky
　　falls into that salty well, grief
because, just because.

An aged statesman sitting
　　with quiet obstinacy by
　　　　his domestic rice-pot –
　　　　Joseph Conrad wrote that, yet what
　　I hear is a voice that's too wry
for the Pah, splitting

hairs. Near bankrupt, I looked out
　　from the castle turret, master
　　　　of nothing I surveyed.
　　　　The material world betrayed
　　my finer feeling. Disaster
passed *really* devout

friends who searched the horizon
　　for the sun and then the Father –
　　　　as an unholy ghost
　　　　I felt like the devil's riposte
　　to them. If creditors gather
the garden's barren.

I can't get clear of that swamp
　　Waikato Valley. And mud sticks
　　　　whichever land you're from,
　　　　whatever one was promised. Rome
　　and Heaven show realpolitik's
claims are paid out, pomp

and circumstance colour both.
 Portraits fade from more than the sun.
  What we conceal reveals
  the most about us. Our ideals
 and our contingencies are one
delusion, the truth

suffices: 'I will survive.'
 Yet no one does. We must render
  unto Caesar not God
  for a lifetime, riding roughshod
 over every doubt, our tender
thoughts buried alive.

2   *After 22 March 1888*

In black gym rompers, Mary
 and Claire Ross polish saints' haloes
  in sure and certain hope …
  When you're ten it's more than a trope –
 if nuns always wear underclothes
that is modesty.

At Thursday's confessional,
 with an accent sharp as a burn,
  the priest forgives each girl
  who made a leap of faith to twirl
 before a carpenter's son: 'Learn
the Roman Missal.'

Head and heart one when you're dead
 if not gone, I want to believe
  as Mary and Claire Ross
  believed when they were ten. The cross
 rosary and lesson deceive
those easily led

astray. But why *I* am here
    disturbs their circle. 'There's no time!'
        I complained while alive
        and I was right, some of us thrive
    in Eternity, the sublime
and final frontier.

Ghosts inherit the moment
    because the moment's everything.
        If you participate
        in a story, then you create
    more than you thought. By burying
cliché, you're fluent

in the future that is now
    a car-park. God is ironic.
        Our ignorance is real –
        we hold a few parts but we feel
    this can't be the whole: Platonic
forms might teach us how

one thing in general is
    many things in particular
        and that's universal.
        Creation is the dispersal
    of matter; x then y are there –
or that's what God says

when He's not resting. God knows
    what orchid blooms ahead of us,
        we still smell it. Formless
        as the night at new moon, I guess
    nothing becomes everything, plus
the First Cause. Suppose

Panentheism holds good –
        does that mean judgement's suspended
                like the globe in nothing
                and its darkness? Without judging,
        that no soul ever ascended
 when, misunderstood,

God chose to keep His distance?
        In the midst of life we are in …
                In *Martin Chuzzlewit*
                the barber must pay a visit
        to the baker; he can't explain
why. Our existence

is conditional on what
        cannot be seen, the Holy Ghost –
                I should feel empathy.
                The visitors to TSB
        Wallace Arts Centre spend at most
an hour to allot

the judgement that God withholds.
        'It's not what you think …' I over-
                hear an earnest father
                reassure his son. Consider
        'The Preparation' by F4
Collective: the folds

in the left hand of a girl
        taped to her mother's back, the folds
                in the mother's shoulders
                barely there, while a boy smoulders
        to the left, as if he upholds
the law. Fingers curl

around this stanza: *I say*
    what happens here. Father and son
        leave the gallery, lost
        for words. Some works of art accost
    you like streetwalkers; this is one,
it changes the way

you think about family –
    mine is scattered, blood in ferment
        underneath the singsong
        of birds and cicadas. What's wrong
    with this is *me*, the sentient
relict who should be

sleeping. If I face both ways
    I own nothing and it makes me
        an inarticulate
        diarist who mistakes the date
    and skips detail – that repartee
we use to fill days

when the rain is a blanket
    over the shivering children
        Monte Cecilia
        schools for the life to come, whether
    or not it does. Yes, there and then
destiny is set.

It appears impersonal.
    The fully moral do not reach
        an house not made with hands
        after following God's commands.
    Redemption's beyond parts of speech –
it's a miracle

language gets us anywhere.
    As children learn to twist and shout
            sound follows the body,
            it describes a space that's godly
    if sweat blood and tears are devout
attempts at prayer,

if they're not then what matters?
    We're lost. I got lost, a voyeur
            searching for the moral
            to *my* story. The law is null
    and void, a sort of erasure.
Every day shatters

the dream and we lose pieces
    as we go. I pick up the odd
            shard of laughter at Pah
            when visitors share their bizarre
    impressions of art; while they nod
knowledge *de*creases

with each word that's overheard
    on the polished stairs. Divided
            states, split infinitives
            make for chaos. Whatever gives
    grace to us, it is presided
over by the word

or so it's said. With suitors
    girls move through the garden like light
            and they fade as quickly.
            When I say 'Adieu!' the turkey
    oak shadows me. I feel contrite
and stupid, the cause

of it all, but what is *it*
 exactly? Immeasurable
   like the current between
   an ellipsis' stepping stones … Seen
 but not heard, children are able
to tell: they admit

nothing about love, the rest.
 Here I am trying to control
   detail others ignore:
   There is no work, nor device, nor
 knowledge, nor wisdom in Sheol,
whither thou goest.

So many things disappear
 in the horseshoe of a river
   or the turn of a phrase.
   It won't matter how long we gaze
 at the vanishing line, whether
love will persevere,

we'll break on the wheel, *Rota*
 Fortunae. We're indifferent
   as the stones in a wall
   to the idea of freedom, all
 most of us know is argument
about our quota

of sex, drugs and rock'n'roll.

[19.11.2014–25.1.2015]

Instead of, in Memory

Reverend Leicester Kyle (1937–2006)

Inside church a whistle is defiant, outside
inviting – after service girls
show their legs and then some, mounting
bicycles, they circle
the hedge of masculine and feminine
rhyme: *grief, belief.*

We go after certainty, slurring our words
we hum like generators yet power nothing
to speak of, we can't
wait to grow up under the stars –
the stars leave us
smaller than ever.

[31.7.2010–25.8.2012]

Family Secrets

1 *The sky is for migratory birds*

'The soil is poor, over the road
they mow whatever grows.' The pram pulls Mum
indoors. 'We leave the front for the kids to kick a ball.'

Her floral blouse fills the kitchen with perfume, eternal
return – bench sink bench oven bench, she works in her own shadow
the sun is in the centre. 'Can't see us getting there.'

In his judder-bar voice, Dad pulls up Mum:
'It's good enough for the likes of us.' Awake
to the dream of a state house, the sound of an egg beater inside that dream;

on orange formica, the second-best tea set; three ducks above a coke fire
steaming smalls. My sister plaits her hair –
'Fuck, let's go to the shops so someone will talk to us.'

When you're *nearly* sixteen swearing becomes prayer.
Filling the front yard, winter sheets are sails
catching the slightest yet trembling -ing -ing

2 *Pass your mother the gravy*

Mother, hold that tongue, hold
your man's juice until the egg cracks
yes, then
pour his also-rans
into the iron pan of marriage;

reduce the never-to-be
to a sticky glaze, taking care
to stir with laughter, however bitter.
Red wine will help
the guilt.

3   *Bottled up*

The jars of pears my mother preserved, they preserve her
for me: hide and seek in the pantry, shadows growing
over floral linoleum,

                    blood not altogether scrubbed off
when her strapless sandals caught the force of falling
seasons, *Spring 1969 Summer 1970* …

                          My vision must be peripheral
if our knowledge is partial, the size of a hazelnut
held before my father disappeared, she limped after.

[15.10.2011–16.3.2016]

Fitting

for Bill McDowall

In the corner shop there are no shoes to compare;
I like the old guy well enough but his business ones pinch.
Besides, I'm an artist. Red leather, blue suede.

My Uncle Bill used to make them. I want a pair
from the summer of 1969, when he was happy.
They will be my dancing shoes. The buckles must shine.

[29.8.2013]

24

The Impossibility of Strawberries

Once a dress the colour of sunset. After dark she would let him
take it off. Even the god who approved could not watch.
'If you want love to stay, shut up
our house, covering the furniture with dirty sheets.'

When the moon was full he could see it in the pond.
Still, if he pulled the shutters there would be no colour, just
the memory that is language, bad language.
He could have married the younger sister with the swan's neck

who said: 'When strawberries are fresh why write about them?
There is already more darkness than you know.
Don't offer me shadows when I need strawberries.'

He didn't care. Only later, the later that takes him into old age.

[24.4.2013]

Being Prepared

As if all the children inside us hit one another …
Where the windscreen had been there was wind,
invisible yet concrete. Even if I could not touch it
I was touched.
                    Each piece of information carried
the same weight: there is blood
on her collar, the dry grass is going to seed
beneath a rain cloud.
                    Then the bees appeared.
I lay their corpses upon the trolley; they spill
onto a parquet floor, upsetting its pattern.
I take care to keep the doorways clear for our children.

[3.3.2012–9.9.2012]

Venture My Word

for Philip Matthews

1

on the verandah
barefoot, I verify
the line of sandals
there is order, it is
exterior: I thought
the known world
at my disposal

where the children sit
outside the green door
a pile of newspapers
contingent on what's
there, I'll watch
from a secret place: this self
is it imaginary and what if

it disposes of me
and you, the reader
we both go west
with the sun, another
symbol of the centre
where every thing
made sense for one day

the news is really about me
'without whom …'
there being no alternative
player with ups and downs, once
measured by our step
between flesh and spirit
day one was a rainbow

2

on the verandah
I recognise whatever
disappears: you
for instance, secure
in your father's armchair
reading this: me too
a cliché, really

where the children sit
in the circle of purpose
raid the unspeakable
in the love of God
forgiving infidelity
beautiful through inclusion
'all creation is groaning' (St Paul)

we share a pronoun
we become one
another: each self

let i = u
by day, by night
complete (in 23 pairs)

twists like a leaf, falls
backwards into the gene pool
filled with possibles:
'I'm waiting for my man'

without fear of falling
through the looking-glass
the selection: let x = y
'I'm so tired, tired of waiting'

[19.10.2012–19.1.2013]

When You Grew Up the Colour Blue was Different

Elizabeth Bishop lived in Brazil; she liked women, you knew
nothing about them, yet. Her poems showed blue,
the inner flame of a Bunsen burner. Then you grew up.

God's favourite colour must be blue; it is the one He chooses to hide
behind. You could say 'window' but the window is
broken, like English, the language most people pretend not to know.

Tea with blueberry muffins, a monogrammed cup upon its
chipped saucer. Elizabeth's scent, only hers, collects
in the collar of your coat. Soon you will speak Portuguese.

[20.4.2015–4.9.2015]

The World of Letters

1   G.M.
Writing is the objectification of memory –
'a fatality in a dressing-gown' (Nietzsche)
in the small hours, when even a mouse is comfortable
under the hot-water cylinder.

Saying is only one way of doing, it is
a narrow cloth for a long table.
However hungry, everyone must leave table
without much thought for the stained cloth.

2   J.B.
After you said everything there was more.
Your sentence was not long enough.
The thing a word touches becomes less
tangible, nowhere near
                                    the world you know.
As if *it* was going to fit inside your head.
As if the lake and the lake's reflections
included you. Everything said meant nothing
once the duck steadied itself and landed

leaving this sentence on the surface.

3   M.H.
When there is no question left, then we have the answer. Instead this
multiplicity of connections, the net tangles and drags us down, so far
below speech we cannot hear an echo, no self to circle with words, how
can this be? Hardly an answer, that bubble coming to the surface so
searchers will know where we are, when we were.

4   I.L.

You hold her as if she was water, water that holds you up.
As Valery said 'Lusitania, too, is a beautiful name.'
Swim inside the shipwreck
that is language, picking through the galley's best bone china.

5   A.C.

You would snap a line to find the world's circumference,
it sounded like a wedding band.
I'd sooner trust the string around a bird's ankle.
What comes with age is shame, language finds
a swallow's nest is made of mud and saliva.

[10.7.2012–15.5.2016]

The Speak House

How am I to tell you the terrible news that my beloved son was suddenly called home last evening.

*   At six o'clock he was well, hungry for dinner, and helping Fanny to make a mayonnaise sauce; when suddenly he put both hands to his head and said, 'Oh, what a pain!' and then added, 'Do I look strange?' Fanny said no, not wishing to alarm him, and helped him to the hall, where she put him in the nearest easy-chair. She called for us to come, and I was there in a minute; but he was unconscious before I reached his side, and remained so for two hours, till at ten minutes past 8pm, all was over.*

– Margaret Isabella Balfour Stevenson to her sister,
Jane Whyte Balfour, 4 December 1894

Fines: $ 1 dancing
            $ 5 weapons (concealed)
            $15 murder
            $25 stealing
            $50 lying

At Maraki old men value the word
yet nautical charts are made of sticks: straight,
curved, caught by a yellow cowry
that is an island. Wind-stick, current-stick point
the coast. One sail is two days, two sails one.

If it rains they say a star sparkles. The tide swells
like an accordion playing hymns, God
the Father asks after His family
without waiting for an answer.
The trophies of the dead questions the living beg,

far more than weapons are concealed.
Instead of a seagull its shadow on the shallows.
Each moment is green, the green grows
darker as our years float past Maraki
towards an uncharted reef – or Treasure Island.

Each white sail is a low cloud, surreal
the shout from the mizzen shrouds:
'One more step, Mr Hands, and I'll blow your brains out!
Dead men don't bite, you know.'
Fine: $15

At Vailima races are more mixed than crops
but less trouble to cultivate.
'Lord, that man does not belong
yet.' We nail civilisation into place
with memory, then forget it. *Pālagi*

tins of kerosene, barrels of salt beef
lean against palms; we weed the yard
and call that purpose. I expect a pet dodo
to pick at the dark tapa cloth
above the bed from Hoffnung's.

'Here, you boy, what you do there?
You no get work? You go
find Simile; he give you work. Peni, you tell this boy
he go find Simile; suppose Simile
no give him work, you tell him go way.'

The view is more than *Pālagi* can see.
Rich, we invest in real estate;
the poor give themselves to the real.
They plant at full moon, otherwise
the fruit will be small, it will be ours.

Perfume of bruised peas, sweet
corn, lima beans around a fowl house
caulked with guano like a German boot.
The colonist watches for that golden egg from Aesop.
An axe is on the stone.

'If horse go lame, bind bacon fat
it faster than star. Dye mane with lime, trick devil
it already god.' Globe artichokes grow
where hooves were planted on the path home.
The smell of old leather is not a saddle,

it is a whip. Surrounded by mummy apples
a pullet with its heart torn out –
is it a pullet? The name is wasted.
'Too many devil down here …'
The alphabet cannot contain them.

At Onoatoa the missionary's child called
Painkiller. Simplicity is cynical, a slight
inspiration through the nostrils.
Figs, limes, bananas are articles of faith.
Our congregation sings in a thatched birdcage.

The haggard and hard stagger over psalms
but innocents have perfect pitch.
(Heaven is the home where tired children go;
they stroke one another's hands, following
the heartline. Then they sleep forever.)

The Catholic mission is coral, roof tied to sky
with sennit and extinct birds' feathers.
The native girls, their brilliant dresses
flower on the cliff. Yesterday they slipped on clean shifts,
clouds were white – now the horizon's hem

frays like servants' nerves: 'Bullimakaw
too bloody hot by roadside, too much
shine in sky.' Out of place
the shouts of the damned, who are frantic
unloading their cargo of bones

at Saluafata Harbour. The soul trader learns from weather,
he accepts good and bad, questioning
what's constant. When those native girls are most tempting
in early evening, sailors go on the promise of a kiss
yet spend midnight alone

with their eyes open, afraid to love
too much. 'Look at me – I no got belly
allee same bullimakaw!' Squall succeeds squall
before the harbour is calm, the pilot sees
clear to the next world …

The dream that is stronger than death is common;
it does not belong to the feverish solitary.
It is literature, milk sprayed from a priestess' mouth
over the corpses of political appointees, business leaders
and those whose lungs they coated with tar.

The dream that is stronger than death is owned
by the Samoan who kneads dough, Peni. It is owned
by the poor white who breaks bread
to share with his brother, Simile. It is owned
by the half-caste who untangles the net of words –

the eel of belief is caught in the net, its tail sustains
more than one True Church. With its mooring rope
shorter than an eel's tail,
where will this white man's boat go? Tagaloa-lagi,
don't borrow mystery from Christians like me.

The sea takes the raindrop because it must;
that does not mean each soul is predestined.
My hunting dogs don't bark because they want to know
right from wrong – they bark for meat.
The leaves do not rustle because they are uneasy.

If the ship's pilot has lice in his hair, then wind ruffles it
regardless – wind has no regard for society, it is an anarchist
like Rimbaud in Java, Gauguin in Tahiti.
And words are shifty clouds, they replace what was
solid, they refuse to mean what we think yet leave us

free. The rebel chief Mataafa's men dream of saying
whatever comes into their heads, godly
when they step onto the crate of spirits.
Perhaps words are nocturnal, it is safer to travel
when informants can't follow …

Look, on Apia's side streets there is censer's smoke.
An ironist, the gendarme leads his horse.
He will arrest happiness, it is a vagrant
on the corner of two centuries.
The priest pretends we must choose right or wrong.

Brothers fight on opposite sides;
it does not matter who wins –
each keeps his property. Time is lost.
How to account for it?
By straining kava into a bowl.

The worth of a servant's work is fixed,
the worth of a white man's grace is fixed
by blood. Dawn arresting, always
the shackle of earth's curve fits an ankle.
Thigh-bones are collected for the life to come, here

pubescent girls understand what blood can do.
The seven acts of mercy are sexual.
They cannot be buried by dogma.
We remember living, we do not
remember living without dirty words.

With the open mouth of a wooden god
an old man knows if your fish is caught by the lower jaw
your girl shares her bed with a ghost.
After she pours cold water, her nipples.
'Are you kind?' Nod but say nothing, the nothing

that must be said. If she grows heavy
blame the angel of the annunciation, shirt
tucked firmly in a fresh pair of trousers.
– That is the young sailor's credo.
His coat black as lava, smile tight as a jailor's handshake

Captain Smollett walks with Squire Trelawney
on the leeward side, out of the wind
but the sea is a hacksaw
and its teeth wear the leg of a cook, Long John Silver.
'He'd look remarkably well from a yard-arm, sir.'

The bloody moon could turn yellow as a condemned man
when warders bring the priest. We hope the moon will go on
beyond knowing, dreary, yet somehow lovable.
The body doubles because the heart, my God!
And the head cannot mark eternity.

Seas are light despite the dark above, the dark
below. Sure enough, the sun.
We see the pilot surrounded by white
bones. He must be the afterlife
of the child who used to skip stones. Let be, let be

poetry of the inconsequential, hope that wraps
a birthday present. From Mulinuu Point to Matautu
the voices of petitioners break in waves:
'We do not understand.' Silent swimmers
let the sun mess with their shadows

near shore. Between sea and swamp that will be sea
the people, 70% water. They sail
inside the reef, through purple
passages from travel guides. Ink stains
my outstretched hand. It is dark.

'Me too muchee 'fraid, no sleep, no can
alleetime same cold.' Blinds woven
coconut fronds, light
broken coconut fronds. *Yo ho ho.*
'Too many devil down here,

they make stink from mussa-oi, ylang-ylang
hide salmon, devil like
with blood young woman.' *And a bottle of rum.*
Tumble down Mount Vaea
wrapped in Queen Victoria's damask …

Mrs Stevenson senior says she 'will not be left
to pray with only servants'. I am afraid
that distinction is not made in other quarters.
Mother, my head is a rotten nut
crumbling under the pressure of Edinburgh's air.

I see that Lutheran, Lucifer, dries tobacco on a rack
improvised from crosscut saws. *Yo ho ho.*
And there is the centre of Europe, the mirror.
'War come sure now; that no thunder, that
devils fight up in sky. Mean war come quick.'

Mataafa's knife scrapes the rust from cartridges.
Laupepa's government will be a basket of heads.
Starlight strikes the dead and the living
with equal intensity, flesh being what it always was.
Flies shine where stars fail

in the join of bandage and ulcer, my head
spins with the world that is beyond
me, there must be something I'm not
doing. Dawn is dusk, fire somer-
saults Vailima blistering Meissen from Dresden from Edinburgh

here. Good God there must be something.
No pilot can see over the horizon no
Samoan locks my father in a light house
so I float alone in the row boat
Treasure Island nowhere. Mataafa told me:

'If man no shadow no man.' I go west,
leave my youth on the east coast
stored between two canoes
beyond high tide. I run over
the hill where Mataafa's ancestors guard clouds.

As a boy in Edinburgh the sky was always
falling on my head. Pollarded
trees hollow as they grow. Tagaloa-lagi,
I don't feel a thing, breathless
running after my shadow: that is what writing is.

If you spit a cherry stone then don't expect victory
in a wrestling contest, you have to practise
your hold on a shadow.
A rusty fishhook is not a lot of use;
cast until your arm is a shiver. Cast farther than this world

I told my self, in Rome the basilica has broken its shoulder.
In Wittenberg there are ninety-five shards.
In Upolu there is a fisherman's story,
the northerly that lifts roofs and eyes
to the charred sky. For God's sake pay attention.

Yo ho ho. Send ahead your voice, when it goes faint
it can rest in an empty water-trough. There are no horses left.
Laupepa's warriors spooked them, then the warriors' ghosts.
It may be too late to reinforce 'the window of the soul'
with shutters made from local timber. 'Devils fight up in sky.'

Storm, conjunct roar of our gods,
go to France, find Loia.
If he is not there search the visible world
then the invisible world
for our brother. Carry him back by high tide.

Storm, if there is an abscess on Loia's leg
don't lance it with a dirty fishbone
or poison will spread through his body and beyond,
your clouds will become pustular,
bursting over Samoa instead of Tonga …

It is not as if an island rises from the sea
to accept the dead, *Sonate pathétique*
honouring a mix of animal scent and sandalwood.
It is not as if the flower behind a widow's ear
listens for the scent of her ancestor, for

dripping lianas. Yet it has come true,
the promised land is underfoot.
Sun stuck on the treetops, love
tangible in the detail of being
here, firstborn and fresh

as every morning. I expect to see
a Christmas tree, handmade stars
hanging over bags of sweets
from an Edinburgh confectioner.
I expect my father will arrive, laughing.

Once Mataafa asked: 'You believe
things are in English?'
I replied, 'English is the lichen
crumbling that rock it tries to hold
in the name of …'

When I went into silence, then
he could follow me. Everything made
makes sense. When I said
nothing, he saw the thing
rather than my failure to say it.

The wave never regrets breaking.
It was made to, and you and me …
We must give up what we cannot have
for ever, let the word go
its own way, the way of the echo.

When we stop so does the road.
Except that Vailima is real
when we're not there, however
little breath comforts our lungs
when we hear the last rites

if we hear them, if we follow
the light house on the sea
beyond the bar, beyond
all possibility of *an house not made* …
And then the wave, and then.

[4.6.2013–2.3.2014]

The Vanishing Line

The morning did what mornings do, left us
alone – although 'us' implies some consolation
from gossip, hugs, love of the common. But no

each perception is private, essential, isolating
like a poem, I thought, walking towards
the courtyard. Already I saw the scaffold.

*

A love song is a child climbing a tree
for the first, the perfect time
until the missed handhold.

When we fall it appears our arms push the air
aside, yet all we think of is our selves
falling, *Mother of God!*

It's impossible to right the day
that's gone, the night to come by will
alone, appetite's not quite love but it does for most of us.

What's a kiss? Something that does not take.
Not a wave, then? Yes, a wave
that pulls back.

*

The human is a device that turns itself
first into ash, then into flowers
the ash is a device that turns itself
first into flowers, then into honey
the honey is God's gift to the human.

The optimist believes chance is his servant
the pessimist recognises it as his master
the optimist trusts in heavenly judgement
the pessimist fears earthly retribution
the optimist is surprised to find dirt under his fingernails

the pessimist always knew it was there.

*

The politician promises to kick down the door
the door is open, when it was closed so was his mouth.
The priest believes the gates can be oiled, they're off their hinges
when they were barred he demanded our indulgence.
Whatever, the poet prefers a window.

*

Each night a spider's web grows
it is made of absence.
Between, that is where the poem grows
between the visible, the invisible.
Only the invisible owns every thing
we measure the seen.
The invisible, then. And that spider.

[1.9.2012–9.12.2013]

Trope

'What you cannot see is real,' she said, then
disappeared. It was an old trope
but no less powerful, leaving me
alone, the ground indifferent as ever to each
step towards what *is* not there.

I knew that the fruit was safe to eat when
birds flurried over windfalls; hope
grew larger than the wishing tree
where generation after generation could reach
only the lowest branch, fear

so I bit through to the core.

[29–30.4.2015]

Der Abend

listening to Egon Wellesz

1   Pastorale

sky a head scarf tightening
yard dark like my heart
God has a big strap
and bright eyes, brighter than that Levi's buckle
He calls my name

the smallest letters catch the air
and they change places, not countries
but I want to change my country
by rearranging the letters
they are sharp as ship's nails

2   Angelus

A cellar's bulb is more use than the sun
if you are a drunk, you do not care for detail
unless it is on a label. Strong light will hurt
more than a sermon on the virtue of temperance.

If gratitude is the precondition of joy
a drunk will become happy and then some.
Hungover, still go to hear the sermon.
It's obvious what people want, the obvious.

3   Dämmerstunde

Rain does not discriminate, but
the homeless know its touch most often.
On the merry-go-round you
drag your feet, heel and toe like the Highland dancer
loving the thought of her small breasts

under brushed tartan, loving
what the rain does.

If her gaze is empty expect darkness to fill it.
She thinks of you as a piece of Chinese porcelain:
poised, impossible
to touch, with neither water nor flowers inside.

4   *Wind auf der Heide*
grass overgrown no good
for hiding, icy
as an undertaker's smile

as if I belonged to this field
like dandelion and thistle
as if I could fly like them

white on white, silent
I count each hailstone
a blessing

[7.12.2014–22.3.2014]

They Meet When Destiny Is Still Chance

for Milly Burrows

It's a sign, how the clouds collect
like pebbles on a beach, where
a small boy digs a hole with a scallop
and empties the sea into it.

They met when there was still a chance.
First love was remembered clearly, being
farther from death than any other.
They lived in the fairytale

they would live forever, it was destiny.
Go to sleep, she says, already
tired by his smile. The sea
disappears between their toes.

[12–17.4.2016]

In Memory of Ally Willen

Voluminous
shawl, blue with white
over your head
the Young River.

> *With numinous*
> *birdsong, first light*
> *traverses thread*
> *like the spider*

Without regret,
each memory
water leaves stone
is in passing –

> *and we're left, yet*
> *I can still see*
> *you smile, alone*
> *in early spring:*

you pirouette
around a tree
whiter than bone.
And try to sing.

[1–9.4.2015]

Old Jewish Cemetery

for Adam Horovitz

the dead forget

a fistful of air, starlight   ordering their beliefs
snagged on blackberry   some lines from the Torah

around their family plot   protecting the emptiness
you can hear   soon you'll feel

the kiss of thigh bones

[13.4.2016]

The Mica Pavilion

ARGUMENT

1874: CHANG'E, *Chinese goddess of the Moon, looks down on Tuapeka County, Otago. The miner* AH SING *works a gold claim, in the hinter of Lawrence, with his partner* SAM CHEW LAIN. SAM *provides the capital to work the claim from his income as a hotelier.* AH SING *courts* TIRIATA, *the daughter of* TE KAHA *of Kāi Tahu.* TE KAHA *opposes the match; distrusting Chinese and Europeans, he demands* TIRIATA *marry within the tribe.* TIRIATA *falls into depression and dies of grief; she enters the Underworld.* AH SING, *supported by* SAM CHEW LAIN, *then goes to the entrance to the Underworld on the banks of the Tuapeka River. On advice from* CHANG'E *and her companion* WU GANG, *he attempts to win* TIRIATA *back by singing to* HINE-NUI-TE-PŌ, *who warns him off.* HINE *subsequently agrees to restore* TIRIATA *to the care of* TE KAHA. TIRIATA *argues with her father that, since* AH SING *has saved her, they should be allowed to marry. It is full moon;* AH SING *and* TIRIATA *are reunited under the watchful eye of* CHANG'E.

LOCATIONS
- *The Moon*
- *Tuapeka County: goldfields, Lawrence, Tuapeka River*
- *The Underworld*

CHARACTERS (in order of appearance):
- CHANG'E, *Chinese goddess of the Moon, where she lives in the company of the woodcutter* WU GANG *and a jade rabbit that manufactures elixirs.*
- AH SING, *lover of* TIRIATA, *mining partner of* SAM CHEW LAIN
- TE KAHA *(Kāi Tahu),* TIRIATA'S *father*
- TIRIATA *(Kāi Tahu),* TE KAHA'S *daughter, lover of* AH SING
- SAM CHEW LAIN, *hotelier and mining partner of* AH SING
- HINE-NUI-TE-PŌ, *Māori goddess of night and death, ruler of the Underworld; daughter and unwitting lover of* TĀNE *who fled to the spirit world when she discovered the truth, giving the sunset its red colour, and bringing death into the world by killing Maui.*

- WU GANG, *Chinese woodcutter, exiled to the Moon for seeking immortality; he is allowed to return to Earth if he cuts down a cassia tree there, however it grows back immediately so he can never leave.*

SCENE ONE: Declaring

Setting: Watched by CHANG'E *from the Moon,* AH SING *and* SAM CHEW LAIN *at their gold-mining claim near Lawrence:*

SAM CHEW LAIN (TO AH SING):

What we want is often the death of us.
    I might suffocate under gold
dust. My father drowned in the Pearl River
    trying to recover a lure.
Where there are heroes there are wet gravestones –
        they're overgrown.

It's difficult to know let alone do
    the right thing in a world of things.
A lover's conscience is a Chinese Box.
    Confucius knew that if you hear
you forget; if you see you remember.
        I stand upright.

 That action expands the known universe.
    Look harder, the mountain depends
upon the view adopted: a dark shock
    from base to apex, then the sun.
I throw the shovel over my shoulder,
        spilling raw light.
                        Hours carved out of schist,

minutes splinter into seconds
then milliseconds. Everything gets small
    before the mountains.
                        Look at your hand,
    its lines are short except for one –
the heart, which grows deeper each time you touch
           Tiriata.

AH SING (TO SAM CHEW LAIN):

Despite the smoke of this campfire I stare.
    'Do not lift the knife while you skin
potatoes – these kūmara are sweeter.'
    So I keep the pressure constant
like my love for her, stripping off the skin
           of tradition.

SAM CHEW LAIN (TO AH SING):

Sort your priorities, even the sun
    visits one side of this world first.
Because we lack understanding and means
    we go deep into the mountains,
hoping to gain both. The clouds don't confuse
        a mountain pool.

You go on about the clouds, not the void
    beyond clouds. It is prejudice
that binds our feet, as if we were women;
    it stops us from travelling through
appearances to the real. You must *see*
        Tiriata.

There is a ferry on Ch'in-huai River –
　　each trip is a preparation
for the next. Each breath is for the next breath,
　　then it is for the trip beyond
breathing. We miners dig through to China
　　　　for an echo.

SCENE TWO: *Warning the Daughter*

Setting: Te Kaha *and* Tiriata's *whare, Lawrence*

Te Kaha (to Tiriata):

Women don't have the freedom to be wrong.
　　Scattered firewood does not season;
it will not warm like wood from a bundle.
　　You must stay with us, marrying
among the tribe. Look within the compound
　　　　for your freedom.

Tiriata (to Te Kaha):

　　　　　　Why drink local water?
The leaf stays but the flower disappears.

Te Kaha *glares, then sends* Tiriata *to her room.*
Tiriata (*alone, through a window to* Chang'e, *the moon*):

Chang'e, study this window's strong corner:
　　the vertical line is Ah Sing,
I am the horizontal. And we fit.
　　Because we do others can see

through to another world, where
heads do not shake.

My sisters confirm the seed of all men
sets the same colour on their skin.
I'll fall, a stone at the speed of twilight
through the underworld's black window
until Hine-nui-te-pō catches
what's left of me.

Despairing, TIRIATA *falls asleep. During the night she dies of grief.*

SCENE THREE: *Through the Black Window*

*Setting: The Moon shines over the entrance to the Underworld, near
Tuapeka River (*AH SING *with* SAM CHEW LAIN *outside,* TIRIATA *and*
HINE-NUI-TE-PŌ *inside*):

WU GANG, *from the Moon* (TO AH SING):

When nesting, magpies break from trees
to chase away the storm. There is no nest,
only the storm

and the order behind it. Everything
unfinished, everything finite
except for an informing principle –
love. Open like a Sichuan
fan, the almighty universe expands
into nothing.

I see more than you: soldiers with helmets
made of paper, heroes who tremble

when envoys arrive, silent mendicants
    staring at washerwomen's breasts.
I see clearly like the gods who condemn
      and then pardon.

Chang'e (to Ah Sing):

Some leaves are picked in spring, some in autumn
    but they must steep for the same time
once they are in the Jingxi jar. The dead
    collect around Hine-nui-te-pō
until she dries them and measures their strength
      in a try pot.

Life, a drinking bout on a pleasure boat
    with ponkan honey oranges
rotten in the bowl. Do you have a choice?
    Your fingers will still be sticky.

Sam Chew Lain (to Ah Sing):

We know love is invisible, like air.
    We breathe without seeing what's there.
 We believe. At the river's edge who thinks
    Air is better than this water,
I won't dive in, finding my way by grace
      with my eyes shut?

Let her float without you, clear to the moon
    where Chang'e can teach her to drum
with rabbit's feet. Wu Gang hacks
    at the cassia, it grows back
instantly. He will never leave the moon
      you stare at, mad

for immortality. Trust the tin mug,
    the pinching boots we must pull
off when you drink too much. What is the cloud?
    A dragon's sloughed skin. And the dream?
A rabbit's lucky foot. And the earth we score?
        A meniscus.

AH SING (TO SAM CHEW LAIN):

When the crescent moon stares through a window
    at a mirror, it wants wholeness
rather than surface representation …
    It wants to see what is *not* there.
With Chang'e and Wu Gang, I need to be
        an immortal

and I need my songs to be visitors
    echoing across the border
of time: each moment hosts eternity
    so there is my entrance to death,
in a sustained note, an arpeggio,
        a breathing space.

TIRIATA's *ghost* (TO AH SING):

The executive residence is reserved for God.
    It is not a place we will stay
being Chinese, being Māori. Look back,
    my ancestors set traps for birds.
When white men asked what they wanted the most
        it was to fly.

Perhaps, at night, the morepork calls for you
    the way I call for you all day,
            Ah Sing?

Tiriata's *ghost* (to Hine-nui-te-pō):

If it is true that gods speak through humans
    but not to them directly, why
 let the dogs howl at midnight. But tell me
    who plucked the *qin*, strummed the *ruan*
so the tunes flew into every seashell
       to please children?

Ah Sing told me about these instruments
    as if the nor'wester played them
the way it plays trees, their shadows.
    Why do men bend the straightest branch?
They break it, then pretend it was hollow
      and held a song.

Hine-nui-te-pō (to Tiriata's *ghost*):

Silence is what most people share with ghosts.

Ah Sing (*interrupts* Hine-nui-te-pō):

Every thing has its home: song lives in air
    and the singer who keeps his song –
he's forgotten like the politician
    who promises to deliver
a cartload of presents to the poorest
      but steals the horse.

Together men can invent a language
    to express their grief for the dead,
a language that lets the dead laugh so hard
    they collapse their monuments, throw
stone after stone into the sky, sophists
      who know the truth.

HINE-NUI-TE-PŌ (TO AH SING):

Ah Sing, your songs will hover like wild geese
    over a tidal bore: they'll land
on the dark lake of memory, its mirror
    showing up dead stars. A rainbow
changes with every step, you never see
        the same rainbow

twice. So you'll never get to where you were
    with Tiriata. I learnt this
after I slept with my father, spreading his seed
    as I ran: you cannot return
to first love. If a thing grows, its shadow
        grows larger still.

Infernal cartography has one landmark:
    the heart. It changes for us all
and changes all of us; it cannot be
    fixed, the antechambers fill up
with blood, the same blood that forces you
        to sing through stone.

With little care for the gods who look on
    hungry children make their way home.
They believe they will eat good food
    instead of rotten scraps, and yet
that is what most people will sit down to
        after midnight.

AH SING (TO HINE-NUI-TE-PŌ):

Perhaps my song can heat the earth, turning
    three seasons to the fourth, summer?
When *The Book of Songs, The Book of Music*

and *The Spring and Autumn Annals*
all inform this thought, then you will listen
      and let the dead go.

They will reappear like perennials
    in ceremonial gardens,
like dock on the scarp above miners' claims
    after a night of nor'westers.
Tiriata will dance through the valley
      with her shadow.

[*Hearing* Ah Sing, Hine-nui-te-pō *relents and restores* Tiriata *to her father's whare. Before* Ah Sing's *eyes* Tiriata *slowly vanishes as she reaches out for him.*]

SCENE FOUR: *The Birthday of Flowers*

Setting: Te Kaha's *whare, Lawrence*

Tiriata (to Te Kaha):

This is the birthday of flowers. They bend
    around the broken wheelbarrow,
hide a forgotten hoe, break through brambles
    into the sun, like me. Ah Sing
laughs, 'A divine dragon will show its head
      but not its tail.'
               Neither bird nor cage,
the moment won't fly yet it cannot hold.
    If my conscience is a small square
filled with passers-by, then at least one stays
      to talk, Ah Sing.

If Hine-nui-te-pō heard Ah Sing
    you can hear me: the lightest seed,

like aroha, is carried the farthest
   on a strong wind.
                       Let your prejudice go,
   it is an obstinate pig dog
that cannot feed the tribe; it does not see
         the short-cut home.
                           Father,
to see the sunset without shivering
   you must wear more than one layer;
if you are my outer garment, Ah Sing
   sits next to my skin. He warms me
more than a cloak of kiwi or kererū
        feathers. Let go.

TIRIATA *and* AH SING (*who steps forward to join her*):

It is the role of two tributaries
   to converge. The murky water –
it soon clears, reflecting universes
   whichever way it turns.
We make things *mean* by seeing through
       and that is love.

CHANG' E (*looks down at* AH SING):

As if the Chi Yellow Liao Yangzi
   Hei and Huai Rivers converge
in the Sea of Tranquility, as if
   the centre of Heaven and Earth
held itself without tension for all time
       tenseless, perfect

as if. Where a shout is without echo
   because distance is illusion,

when measurement proves impossible, then
    love will be eternal. Ah Sing,
the frog carries its own drum: so do you,
        it is the heart –

it beats constantly. It beats constantly.

[1.2.2013–14.3.2014]

View

tell it like it is, as if
among one hundred dark things
a-quiver in the vanishing

like blades of grass

Finder

we take our bearings
from blue herons
line after line, a-quiver

they're turning

[14–20.10.2014]

What the Four Winds Said

'I want to be a tuneswept fiddle string that feels the
master melody and snaps.'

–Amedeo Modigliani

There is no willow. A violin string, a bow
trail in the river. One more gust must deliver
    the whole concerto …

The gods play too slow, it's difficult to follow
their sustained quiver – we only pick up sliver
    after sliver, so

    we get up and go.

[31.5.2015]

The Soul of Whoredom

There's no call for a party official to point
the moral, all hovels are identical
whether the road leads to Rome, Seoul or Wellington.

Blood might be thicker than water
both fill the gutters. Divided between North and South
the sky grabs at peaked roofs, at soldiers' caps.

I object: I, object. All of boredom is an afterthought
'Me too.' You were the kid
with the skinned knee, the runny nose, the funny haircut

you are stronger than your tormentors now
Anzac poppies take over the promontory, red on red
the afterglow of those gone ahead, so party

you sentient intersection of past and future!

[30.12.2011–1.6.2012]

L'Histoire du Soldat

for Tatiana Shcherbina

Snow, now my motherland belongs to bulldozers
I miss white roses the most
so leave some, secretly, in a jug of holy water.

The wall where I fell was not a ruin, I did not call
Madonna! like a character from Bunin
when I saw an enormous sky.

The heavier the frost the stronger the sun, they say.
Nothing doing, it is chilly as a tax collector's grin
when things don't add up – but nothing does –

it is a perfect circle, a bullet hole.

I believe in ghosts; I don't believe in people …
Not the heroic figure in the tapestry, just one loose thread
pulled under, put up against the wall.

After cleaning the rifle he removed my boots –
were they finer than his coarse-grained leather?
Soon he'll know, going home after dark.

[16–20.12.2013]

Prague Casebook

Schon ist alle Nähe fern
                                        – Goethe

1   *Mr Milner writes from his sickbed*

We turn each page with the deliberation of magistrates
        making sense of the facts as presented, so every sentence
rings in our heads. There it is, the world beyond our parents' gates
        opening so that we can discover the truth, then commence

lying about 'home' … On my 79th birthday, I write
        from Prague, reversing Goethe's dictum: *everything far becomes*
near because the hallway to my bedroom is bright with contrite
        spirits. I expected to hear a bell, instead there are drums.

It's so late. My best overcoat grows thinner after fresh snow
        and the thought of more snow. Even if I have no home, I see
how far away it is. The people here are strangers, they show
        scant compassion; they smile like real estate agents. Honestly,

what am I to do but read an old newspaper? I feel sick.
        The sun is too strong for peacocks. Choose to live in metaphor
and you can make each day over, changing your role; you can pick
        the place where you rest because it will not be real any more.

Our world turns backward, there is no forward unless it is prayer
        but that would be an echo, too. Even judgement is passing.
The best dreams end with the hero riding an ass. Over there
        where I went skinny-dipping in the lake, see how it's glassing

over. Everything we did as kids when no one was looking
        must be corrected by sunset's lens. We remember it then
spin on our heels for home, although we don't know the address. Sing
        Vladimir, sing Osip, to show we are still men among men.

Stalin did not discover zero until he fell in love
  with nothing. Then, whatever the number, he added zeroes
to measure Earth; calculating how to reach Heaven above
  he settled on a pile of bodies. Eventually he rose

as a statue, pointing the way. Today I stare at that statue and recognise
  my ambition as a translator: to own every sentence
passed. I want my version to be the original, my lies
  to convince you they are necessary, even common sense.

Poetry's an alternate universe, and I shape it so
  there is no chaos, only a 'fraternal intervention'
by words on behalf of the Word. (God's favourite word is *go*.
  He found it next to an apple core, but without intention.)

I suppose the ghost is father of the man, and fills our hours
  with an echo of vanishing families who never said
a word against their Lord, although He worked against them with powers
  we can't measure by logic, science, or art. We'll know when we're dead.

I describe the shadow of a leaf, dense as a flock of birds.
  With my right hand I sketch an essay, maybe it's a cartoon
where a man cries as his mouth is filled with dirt instead of words.
  An hour ago the soldiers heard him singing; he's quiet by noon.

As a child he believed in ghosts more than people, now he knows
  every season is simultaneous when you're in heaven
and heaven tastes of dirt. The created world belongs to crows.
  This is a logical necessity, one that is given

by a noun, God. He wanted to say God but the soil stopped him.
  I want to say it but my father holds up his hand, beyond
all reason; worse, beyond these parts of speech, beyond synonym
  and antonym, perhaps mind and body. We can't correspond.

By turning the pages of books, the young summon their parents.
How little they weigh, those nouns, and the verbs do nothing all day!
Plaster falls from the ceiling, yet the dead are outside events.
They no longer want fame; their ambition is sealed in real clay

and it's obvious as an exclamation mark. For God's sake
when I was at Waitaki Boys' High the world seemed eternal
the brass band had always played slow, my father's speeches would take
until the Rapture. I never doubted the force of my will.

Today ended before I had the strength to get out of bed.
My book is forgotten but I have the devil's questionnaire
to hand, and what's left of my prick. Also those things left unsaid
all my life: 'I was wrong, I am sorry, I need you to hear.'

2   *A display case in the Museum of Communism*

What if there are fistfights in the bread lines?
Poetry's half a meal. Don't go hungry.

While people sleep off alcohol on their feet
dream of dancing pumps, a young ballerina's smile.

They used to stay up all night to count tanks
today they stare at your red shirt.

However bold, red is the most fugitive colour.

*

Extract resin from pine trees for turpentine
turning a starling from a swallow's nest.

When it was early birds
circled homeward, from here

we hear a drummer boy.

*

Andrei Stepanovich Arzhilovsky
a boy catches carp with silver scales and a bird's tail.

We are in a world observed by Chagall
and the secret police. If somebody hiccups

it is a denunciation in triplicate. Rat-a-tat-tat!
Tell me about the invisible

Andrei Stepanovich, all the usual hassles
queuing for bread or the grave, saluting

birds of prey: they celebrate Vissarionovich
he rolls the executions on his tongue like berries.

Tell me about the invisible
their gestures are ironic, such a simple thing

the human mechanism:
With this happy life of ours what is there left

not to hurt? Socialism is soup made of cow lips.
Smack smack.

Papa has taken his place with God
Liza is pressing butter at the Collective, Galina

splits stolen timber for both stoves, they took
down Nikisha's barn, they're picking up

the wheat under the floorboards
kernel by kernel.

The starlings disappear, then the stars
yet soldiers march faster in darkness

and sing: 'Alyosha, sha! – take a half-tone lower, stop
telling lies.' The factory's whistle sounds hoarse.

Those shadows are the ghosts of the first Politburo
Trotsky Zinoviev Kamenev Sokolnikov Bubnov

and a small boy with a toy drum, rat-a-tat-tat!

*

The sun doesn't rise for one side of the street
it shines on one side of the street.

When there are strands of long hair
expect an investigation. When there are none

expect an investigation to produce twenty.
Enter that crematorium, the State

where your mother and father must live
with Uncle K. in a filing cabinet.

By the gates two trees stand at attention.
Their leaves have no shadows.

The shadows have been taken for questioning.
Collect the dirt from under

Uncle K.'s fingernails, the dirt
behind Grandmother's eyelids, the dirt

between the toes of the Madonna.

*

In the yard two strangers on opposite sides of a well
looking into the darkness, silent.

After mystery, peace; stunned enemies become friends
because we need one another

to haul up the bucket, to empty our memories into it
each one longer than the tail of a meteorite

then to send the bucket through the night, again.

*

We were assigned a field
to dream, sleeping with one another under stars

their light sharpened the sickles beside us
so, being free to choose, we could

cut the flowers for our funeral.

3   *Mr Milner has a word with God*

It rains harder on the poor. In this storm even your best knots
    slip. Too soon each mother confesses: 'I knew he'd die that way.'
As if a man went to light a cigarette, instead drew lots
    and got the broken match. Joe Stalin loved his mother, they say

he was born that way. For me, it is impossible to tell
    if your silence meant you were frightened when the poor cried out 'Help!'
Whether formaldehyde or pitch, each silence has its own smell
    just as every dog, abandoned, has a particular yelp.

Your paradise was a short ride in a fast car, I got out
    on the wrong side, that's clear as ice on the highway at first light.
No one is above you, nothing is forgotten, so I doubt
    you will spare any of us a long walk into endless night.

[1.3.2016–6.4.2016]

Because Love Is Something Left

Andreas Reischek in Aotearoa 1877–89

I no word holds its thing true

At the threshold
the hardest step
falters. We're told
every controlled
leap from precept
to proof is old

news. If we could
exhale darkness,
spit out falsehood,
becoming good
for something, less
misunderstood

in this dark wood!
But we grow cold.

*   all the devils doing their best

the continual
cloud mantle, midgy
air, suddenly

going home through
disorder, this warm
night

the new moon
stoops to get through
the hedge gate

you understand
the language, beyond
where we wait

your work seems just a useless accumulation
one spray of ivy 'a thing of beauty'
in the perpetual ironic

whirl, these words unheard, these words

* **a whirlpool of small fusses**

Like a dog yowling outside
the shut door, you were frightened –
not by night but by the gaslight's shadow.

Now you live outside your self, a fire-
fly circling the garden's secret
after each leaf steals a piece of sunlight.

* **remembering the fairytale**

Whistle, a dog must come.
But it is not your country, ideal
like Paradise, no woman
moves all the muscles in her face

here for you. There are names to say;
names meant to terrify yet comfort
the way a fairytale does
before we lie down to sleep.

* **love is but one**

Small windows in fish-scale shingles
cut up this country, gorse hedges border the Almighty
the church congregation sounds louder, picking up

English as if it was a decoration, hanging
off the Christmas tree …

Eventually every Presbyterian weatherboard
splits, what lasts is the word rather than the thing
yet the clearest sentence becomes uncertain
if the wind goes in no particular direction.
You need a blanket and pull

the sky over the field where you lie.

*   **the hardest step**

Waterfall all ice, the north wind no lover
            and you must talk through prayers
    in a half-empty church, hearing echoes
            so three tenses become one: the past.

Across the lake cloud, across your hours
    darker cloud. The word 'steady' refers
to rain instead of the memory
    where you live. Winter begins again
and again the heavy step cracks ice.

The lake frozen, the young man stranded
            and no rescue planned –
how it is at fifty-seven, when the heart murmur
            forgets the prettiest girl.

*   **sheets crisp and welcoming as**

frost, frost brighter than the skies
lovers look to with uncertain eyes.

While sheep are boiled for tallow
we fail with the Irish potato –

our hearts are dark and so cold
in Paradise's virginal mould.

*   **despair, that accumulated product of past**

labour, you made it your capital – the great wrong
place where everything hurts, pig dogs
tear at the horizon.

The moon cannot preen itself in a pocket mirror;
it crosses from one side to the other, slow
and sure. A greenstone needle sews riverbed to moon.

But the human world is reduced to a church-pew;
stooped bodies wanting release from confusion
as if there were more. As if 'here' meant 'there'.

*   **breaks but not with day**

In the cemetery scarlet
fever declares its census:
Suffer the little children to come …

Your mouth organ's trill floats over
rātā blossom. Stop
the catalogue of what has gone

west, ice-axe aneroid compass lie
covered in dust, Andreas
and rats must decide what to do.

*   at Moeraki the chief's daughter rides

astride like a man, a Māori
pulls a Chinaman's pigtail: What's this?
The Chinaman traces a tattoo: What's that?
Māori do not care for your name

it is an excuse in a confusion of trees.
In Auckland you were the big noise
here moreporks are stronger.
What smelled was intent

gone rotten, the contents of holds
loaded with imperatives
in London, a whirlpool of small fusses
sucking under our country.

*   the moon is cracked

a whirlpool of small fusses, the fantail's pirouette
clips *aesthetic* into *ascetic*
an echo honours more than its source

tuataras share their burrows with Bonaparte's shearwater
yet every turn of the river there's a serpent
eating that moa's egg the moon

yesterday's sun swept into the Northern Hemisphere's blue
into the gentlemen's clubs of London and Vienna
the sun covered in tattoos

the sun that is beyond you
your name a suit from last summer's clearance
too tight for exercise or rest, Andreas

extract brain and intestines, stuff the stomach with seaweed
bind the body of the text in a sitting position
smoke then set within the cleaving tōtara

to honour Queen Victoria

*   **the taxidermist's watch**

A taxidermist does not take his watch
apart, he winds up the spring all winter
until the crystal is fixed like a gaze
on one thing, the absence of motion
inside, the stopping of time …

When Death has left a taxidermist settles
down with the broken – 'of no fixed abode';
the taxidermist toasts an empty chair
and the shadow of an empty chair
then checks his watch, *God, how late you are.*

II apostrophe

Taxidermy was one way to work
    out the world's uncertainty, sin
        and redemption; to show
        what only God could know
    for all time. Your indiscretion
shirking the valour of a young Turk,

almost a foil for Emperor Franz –
    my people are strangers to each
        other; they are not sick
        at the same time – you pick
    through carcasses that cannot teach
the purpose of Creation is man's

aggrandisement. When the museum
    backlights our divine evolving
        then a child's eyes widen
        sizing up the swamp hen
    under the moa's shadow. String
and scissors deliver God's kingdom

for one Sunday afternoon. Suppose
    God forgives what He does not know –
        mud is luminous black
        to an insomniac
    and fortune teller. You show
love is what taxidermy sews

shut, the guts of the matter removed
    so beauty is lasting, it's held
        between the head and heart
        by memory, the part
    you lose through age. God's law upheld
through love, the one thing time has improved

although it's not a thing, what is left
   but the form in a display case?
      You intuit the soul
      through every animal
   impulse, which man cannot embrace
unless he effaces memes bereft

of sense: you give Creation its face
   with arsenical soap on bone
       and glass eyes that reflect
       the world they can't inspect
   any more. Perfecting skin tone
with vegetable dyes, you can trace

genesis. Penknife pliers forceps
   set aside, the finished display
        moves viewers to ask why
       they see nothing but sky
   when searching for the First Cause. Say
the nothing they see is the vortex

of the Lord, conceptual not flesh;
   then every exhibit is proof
       there is more than thin air
       overhead. And that's where
   faith follows the rainbow. Aloof,
our saviour's silence may enmesh

everyone, leaving us *dead-alive*
   as Gerard Manley Hopkins writes;
       exile from God is hell
      and that's original
   sin. In his heart each sinner fights
through the stinging snow, its afflictive

heat, he reaches a closed museum
    to wait upon those granite steps
        until opening time,
        eternity. Sublime
    yet ridiculous, our concepts
plot infinity to kingdom come …

And the taxidermist turns the world
    around, setting upon granite
        frayed from the precipice
        a moth, its chrysalis
    discarded as an iterate
of form and function. Each flower, unfurled,

through repetition proves it's unique
    while indebted to the dead: you
        present the evidence
        in a cabinet, hence
    your sacred duty to accrue
samples from around that earth the meek

inherit. Perfection is striving
    for perfection, and quantity
        counts, surmounting our doubts
        about design that sprouts
    with the flower. Yet entropy
sends every petal west. Surviving

the world requires more than contriving
    a diorama of delights
        for the blind, deaf and dumb.
        To enter kingdom come
    we must recite more than last rites
because perfection is striving.

As if sin must become man's substance
    blasphemy is a sacrament
        that damns us to order;
        irony marks the border
    between free will, judgement
while God operates from happenstance

or malice. A confiscated book
    the self is obscure; almost lost
        behind rhetoric's veil
        contradictions assail
    our pathetic fallacy, Christ –
although 'our' suggests a second look

in Caxton's *The Mirror of the World*
    'lyke as a flye goth round aboute
        a round apple', sounding
        out our doubts. And we bring
    a bold approach to the devout
life, we follow the leaf as it's twirled

by wind and an invisible will
    until we understand in black
        and white – that's what we know,
        a blank page, the verso
    in our family almanac.
Taxidermists do not have to kill.

Wading across the Avon River
    you forget who you are: so far
        for nothing, your object
        unclear. Too circumspect
    for those who demand an answer
from every anthemic endeavour

you hear Māori, were they ordered to
    speak? Language is not a mansion
        across from the hereafter;
        if you can hear laughter
    then it may relieve your tension
too, but it won't account for the blue

yonder, where there are only echoes –
    the moored pontoon creaking, hawser
        frayed, its angle wayward
        against the wind. No word
    holds its thing true, author
and audience hear whatever shows

the self to advantage. Things don't choose
    to try on names the way a child
        wears one hat, another
        until the tired mother
    stops that game. She was reconciled
to anger so she knew how to lose

favour. If you feel out of favour
    it is because what you see slips
        the word you give it, proof
        positive God's aloof
    from the universe. Each eclipse
increases the darkness, you waver

and fall into silence while the moon
    frustrates the sun. *Come quietly*
        the universe tells you –
        there are many worlds to
    investigate, your words can't be
the measure, they are inopportune

when time is the space between here, now
the dead are waiting. Say nothing
because nothing is all
that's understandable
if you listen. And what you bring
determines who when why what and how

you are. The dead keep their word.
Yet errors outlast energy;
those who proceed with care
also receive their share
while the rest are in jeopardy –
their eulogies will never be heard

over the absence of a black hole.
You feel there is no eternal
soul. The salmon's battle
upstream, your dog's mournful
call to the crescent moon – these all
tell us nothing will ever be full.

Because the ear is vulnerable
the trembling cling to their deafness
so no poetry goes
in, everybody knows
language's amanuensis
silence instead of original

thought, an outpouring of either/or.
It is impossible to be
born an ancient Greek, so
we moderns must forgo
appeals to authority, we
remember to forget, we explore

as if for the first time. We are blind
    to the Braille of universals
         preferring our garden
         to Eden, we harden
   our hearts because of externals
like colour, yet cannot reach behind

to find the miracle that is home –
    which is why we need a mirror
         reflecting *inner* light;
        what we touch is finite
   and to trust things is an error.
If our lasting home is the genome

then our destination is not Rome
    ('he shold goo so ferre that he shold
        come agayn to the place')
      whenever we retrace
   nucleic acid, it is God
who sets the letters in monochrome.

III what you see slips the word you give it

A rich and summerlike world of colour was all around me,
and yet in my heart I was still longing for the snow of my native
Weihnachten with the customary tree and my loved ones round …
– Andreas Reischek, Christmas 1877

* **place setting**

A stuffed animal is a fortune-teller of sorts:
'What will happen when I leave my body?'
Recall your childhood – every question
another window to be boarded up

against the pressure of a sunset, even
your best friend said nothing
good. The stitches between body and soul fail;
the head falls back, filled with so much dark

the collarbone breaks, after the heart.
Nothing finds its way straight to the light, it
diverts through dust first – *and last*
you add, stitching the moa's skin together

so children can wonder what went on
ahead: 'Where did it go?' they say, racing
from the display to Sunday school, believing
there are still eggs to collect.

* **tableland**

Near Arthur's Pass you pursue
a future of stiff collars;
back in Vienna, your wife
sets out the knives and forks
while you fire, again.

The plumpest duck falls
into the Otira River; your retriever
leaps after: *Caesar* you call
across Austria, moving
through the place settings.

*   **migratory bird**

The past is overcast, you
open negotiations with the full moon; it is resting
in an abandoned nest
near the top of the tallest kauri.

Your wings still ache with the weight of another country;
they give way, compressed
by its absence. It seems Creation's protesting
with you. And God is, too.

*   **behind, where, where**

Don't expect a narrow goat track to go straight
or a star to brighten then
curve your way. Skipping a ravine, the river zig-
zags into the goatherd's gaze
and the fisherman's complaint:
trout bit not for hunger but wantonness.

To go the distance you must be sure of your place
like the exhausted poor.
Salvation is another way of overstaying
your welcome …

*   emigrating on the ship of fools

Your captain is tall and broad as the forest
he sees, he hears no better than an oak
and can navigate like an acorn.
Every sailor is the best at steering
wherever, steering can never be learned
unless you appeal to the heavens.
One moonstruck alcoholic takes the helm
the others mutiny, turning
so the ship cuts a circle, it shrinks then
docks in a bottle; your captain
staggers overboard, calling
for the gods whose names are forgotten.
Is this your first journey south?
With the horizon a smudge
you can't ask the past about the future;
it is an unreliable narrator
and the charts are conflicting.
After the fact, your stories float
home: how a slapstick kea perched
on the barrel of your gun, sunning its feathers
one by one, then you
slipped over the edge of a magenta shadow
among Dusky Sound's leaf-quiver
soused with salt water, you walked
seasons with colic for company
drawing a new conclusion with each breath
desperate for a clear shot –
another kea's wings spread, sun
descending so it all went dark
underneath. You heard your father's voice
calmer than Doubtful Sound's water
although he *is* a ghost, although his axe
broke the morning your mother fell
pregnant with you … He seemed to leap

across the Hauptplatz, calling
like a newsboy to the Virgin of Linz.

*   **a catalogue of transients**

#1 *Unknown Man*
    photographed by Julia Margaret Cameron
preferring this world to Paradise
    swore allegiance to 'the real'
went where you liked, not set by the gaze
    directed your way
descending west, alone
    although 'the soul' held itself in that spell
silence, the skin of a ghost

#2 *My Diary* with no signature, the writer's identity kept
behind a palisade of *I …*
            Yet we know what she wanted
for dinner, how one spoon was lost from her best silver
service, the curse of curly hair under a bonnet
and what a beast *he* was.

#3 One metal cylinder, *Three Blind Mice*
the singer 'unrecorded'.
            You listen to this, unknown.

*   **next of kin**

Late summer forgets spring, who forgets
their heart? Stare into the dark
referents, that shock of wind turning
westerly for an orchard or a churchyard
in the distance, always the distance.

* **down in dreamy scatterment**

Form is not a hospital bed let alone a sepulchre –
it is a conjurer's trick, bringing up
the sun over the horizon. And a shadowing

so you can see the leaf without looking
directly, trace it with your toe although it hangs
over you and all that you hold

valuable, feeling content.

* **because love is something left**

and the body is empty, a basket
forgotten after Sunday's fair

quiet like the fall of grey hair
when you shake your head to forget

love is something left

[1.8.2016–17.11.2016]

Notes

The Ghost of James Williamson 1814–2014

James Williamson (1814–1888) was the son of a Belfast linen merchant; as a boy he went to sea on one of his father's ships. In 1840 he left the sea to set up a general store at Kororareka (Russell), before moving to Auckland where he established both a store and a public house. He then became one of the colonial period's wealthiest speculators in property and a pivotal financier, founding the New Zealand Insurance Company (1859), the Bank of New Zealand (1861), the New Zealand Loan and Mercantile Agency Company (1865), and the Auckland Agricultural Company (1881). When the latter failed in November 1887 Williamson became bankrupt. He died suddenly at his mansion, Pah Homestead, on 22 March 1888.

The poem was the subject of the exhibition 'James Williamson's Ghost' at the TSB Wallace Arts Centre (Pah Homestead) as part of Auckland Heritage Festival 2015. The exhibition was curated by historian Vaughan Yarwood, and contributing photographers were Caryline Boreham, Allan McDonald, Anton Maurer, and Haruhiko Sameshima. Installation was overseen by Nicholas Butler of the James Wallace Arts Trust.

The Speak House

Robert Louis Stevenson is the speaker inside The Speak House. I have taken the common phrase 'my life flashed before my eyes' as a signpost. The feverish tumble of impressions that is this poem occurs in the final two hours of Stevenson's life, either between his words 'Oh what a pain!' and 'Do I look strange?' or after he lost consciousness. Tagaloa-lagi will not tell me more.

This poem orients itself from *Our Samoan Adventure* by Fanny and Robert Louis Stevenson, edited by Charles Neider (London: Weidenfeld & Nicolson, 1956); *The Cruise of the* Janet Nichol *Among the South Sea Islands: A diary by Mrs. Robert Louis Stevenson* (New York: Scribner, 1915), also the later edition edited by Roslyn Jolly (Sydney: UNSW Press, 2003); *The Works of Robert Louis Stevenson* (London: Tusitala edition, Heinemann, 1923–24); and *Miscellanea, Volume 26: The works of Robert Louis Stevenson* (New York: Scribner, 1926). Swollen with detail of RLS's life at Vailima from December 1889 to December 1894, the poem is necessarily shaped by the power plays that divided Samoa then.

> *At the time that Stevenson settled in the islands, the government, while technically Samoan, was actually in the control of the three great powers that had interests there, and which had come to a determination at a convention in Berlin some few years previously. These powers were Germany, England and the United States. Under the convention, Malietoa Laupepa, previously deposed by the Germans, was reinstated as king, and Mataafa, a popular kinsman with considerable claims to the throne, who was especially obnoxious to the Germans, was overlooked and left in the position of pretender. The distance between*

the kinsmen grew as native feelings were stirred under the influence of the occupying powers, and war was continually threatened by both camps.

In Stevenson's judgement a native war would have been calamitous and would only have profited the white officials manipulating the scene. He believed that Laupepa and Mataafa would willingly live in peace if permitted to do so, and it was his notion that Mataafa ought to be given a very high post in the government, to which he believed Laupepa would not object.
– Charles Neider, Introduction, *Our Samoan Adventure*, 20–21.

Maraki: Properly Marakei, now part of the Gilbert Islands, Kiribati; 'the neighbouring island of Maraki, distant about sixty miles' from Butaritari (Makin) Atoll. – Lloyd Osbourne, from Nellie Van De Grift Sanchez, *The Life of Mrs Robert Louis Stevenson* (London: Chatto & Windus, 1920), 155.

'One more step, Mr Hands, and I'll blow your brains out! Dead men don't bite, you know.' – Chapter 26, 'Israel Hands', *Treasure Island*.

Vailima: In December 1889 the Stevensons 'purchased ground for what was to become their estate, Vailima, and left orders to have a patch of jungle cleared and a temporary dwelling built'. – Charles Neider, Introduction, *Our Samoan Adventure*, 12.

Pālagi: Papāalagi, *Pālagi* is the Samoan term for foreigners, especially those of European origin.

Simile: 'Henry is a chiefling from Savaii; I once loathed, I now like and – pending fresh discoveries – have a kind of respect for Henry. He does good work for us; goes among the labourers, bossing and watching; helps Fanny; is civil, kindly, thoughtful; *O si sic semper!* But will he be "his sometime self throughout the year"? Anyway, he has deserved of us, and he must disappoint me sharply ere I give him up.' – RLS, *Our Samoan Adventure*, 32, note 14.

Peni: One of the native servants at Vailima. ' "Peni, you tell this boy he go find Simile; suppose Simile no give him work, you tell him go 'way. I no want him here. That boy no good." – Peni (from the distance in reassuring tones), "All right, sir!" ' – RLS, *Our Samoan Adventure*, 57.

the golden egg of Aesop: Aesop's fable (87) as translated by the Reverend G.F. Townsend: 'A cottager and his wife had a Hen that laid a golden egg every day. They supposed that the Hen must contain a great lump of gold in its inside, and in order to get the gold they killed it. Having done so, they found to their surprise that the Hen differed in no respect from their other hens. The foolish pair, thus hoping to become rich all at once, deprived themselves of the gain of which they were assured day by day.'

Onoatoa Island: The *Janet Nichol* put in there on 14 July 1890.

Bullimakaw: 'In the midst of my most troublous moments three natives appeared and said they had a bullimakaw for sale. The name seemed very appropriate, for it was very difficult to guess whether the animal was a bull or a cow.' – Fanny Stevenson, *Our Samoan Adventure*, 37.

Saluafata Harbour: Between Solosolo and Lufilufi, on the same coast as Apia.

Tagaloa-lagi: The Samoan supreme deity, creator of the universe.

Mataafa: 'Mataafa has declared himself king and has made a stand with an immense number of followers.' – Fanny Stevenson, *Our Samoan Adventure*, 116; 'While I was away, Lloyd [Osbourne] accompanied Mrs. Moors to Malie on a visit to Mataafa. The consuls tried hard to prevent Lloyd going. He was charmed with Mataafa, as everyone but his political enemies seems to be.' – Ibid., 127.

Apia: 'Apia, the port and mart, is the seat of the political sickness of Samoa.' – RLS, *Our Samoan Adventure*, 41.

By straining kava into a bowl: Kava is a fermented drink made from the root of a pepper plant and widely used on ceremonial occasions. '[T]he virgins of the village attend to prepare the kava bowl and entertain them with the dance.' – RLS, *Our Samoan Adventure*, 41.

Captain Smollet walks with Squire Trelawney: The captain and the owner respectively of the schooner *Hispaniola* in *Treasure Island*.

'*He'd look remarkably well from a yard-arm, sir*'. – Chapter 12, 'Council of War', *Treasure Island*.

'*beyond knowing, dreary, yet somehow lovable*': 'Mr Utterson the lawyer was a man of a rugged countenance, that was never lighted by a smile; cold, scanty and embarrassed in discourse; backward in sentiment; lean, long, dusty, dreary, and yet somehow loveable.' – Chapter 1, 'Story of the Door', RLS, *Dr. Jekyll and Mr. Hyde*.

From Mulinuu Point to Matautu: 'The western horn is Mulinuu, the eastern, Matautu; and from one to the other of these extremes, I ask the reader to walk. He will find more of the history of Samoa spread before his eyes in that excursion, than has yet been collected in the blue-books or the white-books of the world.' – RLS, *Our Samoan Adventure*, p. 41.

'*Yo ho ho, and a bottle of rum!*' – Chapter 1: 'The Old Sea-Dog at the "Admiral Benbow"', *Treasure Island*.

mussaoi, ylang-ylang: Fragrant bark and tree (*Canapa odorata*) respectively.

Mount Vaea: '[B]ehind Vailima, on the summit of which first Louis, in 1894, then Fanny, in 1914, were buried.' – Charles Neider, *Our Samoan Adventure*, 108, note 11. 'Vaea Mountain about sun-down sometimes rings with shrill cries, like the hails of merry, scattered children.' – RLS, ibid., 58.

'*… she will not be left to pray with only servants. I am afraid that distinction is not made in other quarters*': 'A fight about prayers is really enough to bring a cynical smile to the lips of a bishop. Mrs S. says she will not be left to pray with only servants. I am afraid that distinction is not made in other quarters. I see again she dislikes the life here which we find so enchanting and is disappointed and soured that she is not able to persuade us to throw it all up and go to the colonies. We have given the colonies a fair trial and they mean death to Louis, whereas this is life and reasonable health.' – Fanny Stevenson, *Our Samoan Adventure*, 129–30.

'*My head is a rotten nut*': 'But there is nothing in my mind; I swim in mere vacancy, my head is like a rotten nut; I shall soon have to begin to work again or I shall carry away some part of the machinery.' – RLS, *Our Samoan Adventure*, 202.

Laupepa: On 16 March 1892 'Malietoa [Laupepa] himself, accompanied by

Laulii as interpreter, and attended by three soldiers dressed in white coats and trousers and armed with rifles and bayonets, visited Vailima. Malietoa also wore white, with long yellow leather leggings reaching above the knee. The "king" stayed to lunch and drank kava with Louis, the latter a sign of good will.' – Charles Neider, *Our Samoan Adventure*, 175.

Meissen from Dresden: The first hard-paste porcelain developed in Europe, produced from 1710 onward and collected by the wealthy.

In Wittenberg there are ninety-five shards: Martin Luther's *Disputatio pro declaratione virtutis indulgentiarum*, nailed to the door of Castle Church in Wittenberg, Saxony, on 31 October 1517.

Loia: Samoan name for Stevenson's step-son Lloyd Osbourne, with whom he co-authored *The Wrong Box* (1889), *The Wrecker* (1892) and *The Ebb-Tide* (1894).

Sonate pathétique: Beethoven's Piano Sonata No. 8 in C minor, Op. 13.

all possibility of 'an house not made': 'For we know that if our earthly house of this tabernacle were dissolved, we have a building of God, an house not made with hands, eternal in the heavens.' – II Corinthians 5:1, King James Bible.

beyond the bar: 'I hope to see my Pilot face to face / When I have crost the bar.' – Tennyson, 'Crossing the Bar', October 1889. I measure this against the prayer: 'Lord, the creatures of Thy hand, Thy disinherited children, come before Thee with their incoherent wishes and regrets: Children we are, children we shall be, till our mother earth hath fed upon our bones.' – RLS, 'For Self-Forgetfulness', Vailima Prayers, *Miscellanea*.

Prague Casebook
This poem circles the character of the New Zealander and alleged spy Ian Milner (1911–1991): http://adb.anu.edu.au/biography/milner-ian-frank-16424

Because Love Is Something Left
Andreas Reischek (1845–1902) was an Austrian naturalist and taxidermist who worked in New Zealand from 1877 until 1889, establishing collections at Canterbury and Auckland museums. He also exported thousands of exhibits to the Vienna Museum of Natural History. This poem echoes Gerard Manley Hopkins, Christina Rossetti and John Ruskin as it measures the tension between theology and evolution, word and world.